THE E-COMMERCE SUCCESS JOURNEY

Unveiling Proven Strategies for Business Growth

RICHARD HALE

TABLE OF CONTENTS

INTRODUCTION

Imagine a world where businesses thrive, entrepreneurs flourish, and dreams come to life. A world where the digital realm acts as a gateway to endless possibilities and growth. This is the world of e-commerce, a dynamic and ever-evolving landscape where ambitious individuals and visionary companies have harnessed the power of marketing strategies to scale their businesses to unprecedented heights.

In this book, we embark on an exhilarating journey, unveiling the captivating stories of businesses that have conquered the e-commerce realm. We delve into the methods, tactics, and strategies that propelled these enterprises from humble beginnings to phenomenal success. Brace yourself for a collection of inspiring narratives, intertwined with practical advice and actionable insights, designed to equip you with the tools needed to transform your own e-commerce venture.

Throughout these pages, we will explore the fundamental elements of building a strong brand foundation. We will discover how defining your brand identity and crafting a unique value proposition lay the groundwork for long-term success. By establishing brand guidelines and understanding the essence of your business, you can create a captivating story that resonates with your target audience, building loyalty and trust.

As we continue our journey, we venture into the realm of website design and user experience. We uncover the secrets of creating an engaging e-commerce website, one that captivates visitors, guides them seamlessly through their customer journey, and ultimately drives conversions. You will learn the art of optimizing your website for maximum impact, harnessing the power of conversion rate optimization techniques to unlock its full potential.

No exploration of e-commerce marketing would be complete without a deep dive into the realm of social media. We uncover the art of leveraging social media platforms to connect with your audience, craft compelling content, and foster genuine engagement. From Facebook to Instagram, Twitter to TikTok, we unveil the strategies that transform casual followers into loyal brand advocates.

But our journey doesn't end there. We delve into the captivating world of search engine optimization (SEO), unraveling the mysteries of climbing the search engine ranks and driving organic traffic to your e-commerce store. We unravel the power of paid advertising channels, such as pay-per-click (PPC) campaigns, and reveal the secrets to crafting effective ads that capture attention and drive conversions.

Email marketing emerges as a potent weapon in your marketing arsenal. We uncover the art of building high-quality email lists, crafting engaging campaigns, and implementing automation and personalization to nurture customer relationships and drive repeat purchases.

Additionally, we explore the realm of influencer marketing, where strategic collaborations with industry influencers can skyrocket your brand's visibility and credibility. We analyze real-life success stories and guide you through the process of building authentic relationships with influencers that resonate with your target audience.

But successful e-commerce marketing extends beyond acquisition. We dedicate a chapter to enhancing customer experience and retention, emphasizing the importance of exceptional customer service, implementing effective loyalty programs, and harnessing the power of customer reviews and testimonials to build trust and loyalty.

Throughout our journey, we emphasize the critical role of data analysis and measurement in driving e-commerce success. We unveil the key metrics to track, introduce you to powerful analytics tools, and guide you in making data-driven decisions to optimize your marketing efforts.

As we conclude our adventure, we recap the key strategies that have emerged from our exploration and provide insights into emerging trends in the world of e-commerce marketing. The future holds exciting possibilities, and with the knowledge gained from this book, you will be well-prepared to navigate the ever-changing digital landscape and secure your place among the e-commerce elite.

So, ready your entrepreneurial spirit, ignite your imagination, and join us on this exhilarating journey as we unravel the secrets to scaling your e-commerce business. The stories of success await, and it's time for you to claim your spot in the digital kingdom. Let us begin.

THE POWER OF E-COMMERCE MARKETING

In today's digital world, the rise of e-commerce has transformed the way businesses operate and customers shop. With the widespread accessibility of the internet and the convenience it offers, e-commerce marketing has emerged as a powerful tool for businesses to reach their target audience and achieve remarkable growth. This book aims to unlock the secrets behind successful e-commerce marketing strategies and provide you with the knowledge and insights to thrive in the competitive online marketplace.

E-commerce marketing, in its essence, is the art of effectively promoting and selling products or services online. It leverages the vast reach and convenience of the internet to connect businesses with customers across geographical boundaries. The potential for businesses to tap into a global customer base is unprecedented, presenting endless opportunities for expansion and revenue generation.

Throughout the pages of this book, we will embark on a journey through captivating stories of businesses that have harnessed the power of e-commerce marketing to achieve incredible success. From humble beginnings to industry leaders, these stories illustrate the transformative impact that strategic e-commerce marketing can have on a business's growth trajectory. By delving into the experiences and strategies of these businesses, you will gain valuable insights and inspiration to apply to your own e-commerce ventures.

However, the world of e-commerce marketing is not without its challenges. The digital landscape is highly competitive, with businesses vying for the attention of a constantly evolving and discerning consumer base. Understanding and overcoming these challenges are essential for success. In this book, we will explore the various obstacles businesses face in the e-commerce realm and provide you with practical strategies to navigate them effectively. From standing out in a crowded marketplace to building trust and credibility with your target audience, you will learn how to develop a comprehensive e-commerce marketing approach.

By the end of this book, you will possess a comprehensive understanding of the power of e-commerce marketing and its potential to transform your business. You will be equipped with valuable insights, proven strategies, and practical tips to enhance your e-commerce marketing efforts. Whether you are starting a new online venture or seeking to optimize your existing e-commerce business, the knowledge gained from this book will serve as your guiding light in the dynamic world of e-commerce marketing.

So, prepare to embark on this exciting journey through the realms of e-commerce marketing. By the end of this book, you will have the tools and confidence to navigate the ever-changing digital landscape and unleash the full potential of your business. Let the stories of successful e-commerce brands inspire you, and the practical insights provided empower you to overcome challenges and achieve sustainable growth. The adventure awaits, as you immerse yourself in the captivating world of e-commerce marketing.

BUILDING A STRONG BRAND FOUNDATION

In the vast and competitive world of e-commerce, building a strong brand foundation is essential for long-term success. A solid brand foundation serves as the anchor for your business, guiding your marketing efforts, and connecting with customers on a deeper level. In this chapter, we will explore the importance of establishing a robust brand foundation and the steps involved in creating a memorable brand for your e-commerce business.

Your brand is more than just a logo or a catchy slogan. It encompasses the values, personality, and essence of your business. It is what sets you apart from competitors and resonates with your target audience. Building a strong brand foundation begins with understanding your business's unique identity.

To define your brand identity, start by clarifying your mission and vision. What is the purpose of your business? What value do you aim to provide to your customers? By articulating a clear mission and vision, you establish a guiding light that influences every aspect of your brand.

Next, delve into the core values that drive your business. What principles do you uphold? What beliefs shape your decisions and actions? Your core values reflect the character and integrity of your brand, and they should align with the expectations and aspirations of your target audience.

Crafting a compelling brand story is another crucial element of building a strong brand foundation. Your brand story communicates the journey, passion, and purpose behind your business. It creates an emotional connection with your audience, making your brand more relatable and memorable.

Developing a brand personality is also key to building a strong brand foundation. Your brand personality encompasses the traits, characteristics, and tone of voice that represent your brand. Are you playful and energetic? Or sophisticated and authoritative? Defining your brand personality helps shape how you communicate with your audience and establishes a consistent brand experience across all touchpoints.

In addition to defining your brand identity, it's important to conduct market research and understand your target audience. Who are your ideal customers? What are their needs, desires, and pain points? By gaining a deep understanding of your target audience, you can tailor your branding and marketing strategies to effectively resonate with them.

Once you have defined your brand foundation, it's time to bring it to life through visual elements such as your logo, color palette, typography, and imagery. These visual elements should be aligned with your brand personality and resonate with your target audience. Consistency is key in building brand recognition and trust.

Building a strong brand foundation sets the stage for your e-commerce marketing success, creating a lasting impression and fostering meaningful connections with your customers. So, let's embark on this journey of brand building and set the foundation for your e-commerce business's remarkable growth.

CRAFTING AN EFFECTIVE E-COMMERCE WEBSITE

In the digital realm of e-commerce, your website is the face of your business. It serves as the primary touchpoint for customers, representing your brand, showcasing your products or services, and facilitating transactions. In this chapter, we will delve into the critical aspects of crafting an effective e-commerce website that not only attracts visitors but also drives conversions and enhances the overall customer experience.

The first step in creating an effective e-commerce website is to ensure a seamless user experience. Your website should be intuitive, easy to navigate, and visually appealing. Consider the user journey from the moment a visitor lands on your site to the point of making a purchase. Streamline the navigation, minimize friction points, and optimize the layout to guide users effortlessly towards their desired actions.

Responsive web design is essential in today's mobile-centric world. With a significant portion of online traffic originating from mobile devices, your website must be fully optimized for various screen sizes and resolutions. Responsive design ensures that your site adapts and displays seamlessly across desktops, smartphones, and tablets, providing a consistent and user-friendly experience for all visitors.

Another crucial aspect of an effective e-commerce website is fast loading speed. Research shows that even a slight delay in page loading can significantly impact user satisfaction and conversion rates. Optimize your website's performance by compressing images, minimizing code, and leveraging caching techniques. This will ensure that visitors can quickly access your content and complete their transactions without frustration.

Visuals play a pivotal role in captivating and engaging visitors. High-quality product images and videos that showcase your offerings from different angles and perspectives can enhance the overall shopping experience. Additionally, incorporate visually appealing design elements and typography that align with your brand identity, creating a visually cohesive and memorable website.

Security is paramount in e-commerce. Customers must feel confident that their personal and financial information is protected when making a purchase. Implement robust security measures, such as SSL certificates and encryption protocols, to safeguard customer data. Display trust badges and secure payment options prominently to instill confidence in your visitors.

Product organization and categorization are vital for e-commerce websites with diverse offerings. Ensure that your products are logically organized into categories and subcategories, making it easy for customers to browse and find what they're looking for. Incorporate powerful search functionality that allows users to quickly locate specific products based on keywords and filters.

Personalization is a powerful tool for enhancing the customer experience and driving conversions. Leverage customer data and behavior to offer personalized product recommendations, tailored offers, and customized content. By understanding your customers' preferences and anticipating their needs, you can create a more personalized and engaging experience that fosters loyalty and increases sales.

DRIVING TRAFFIC THROUGH SEARCH ENGINE MARKETING

In the vast online marketplace, attracting a steady stream of qualified traffic to your e-commerce website is essential for success. Search engine marketing (SEM) provides a powerful means of driving targeted traffic and increasing your online visibility. In this chapter, we will explore the intricacies of SEM and how you can leverage it to effectively promote your e-commerce business.

Search engine marketing encompasses two primary strategies: search engine optimization (SEO) and pay-per-click (PPC) advertising. Let's begin by discussing the importance of SEO in increasing your website's organic visibility in search engine results.

SEO involves optimizing your website's content, structure, and technical aspects to improve its search engine rankings. By strategically incorporating relevant keywords, creating high-quality content, optimizing meta tags, and improving website speed, you can enhance your website's visibility in search results. Appearing higher in search rankings increases the likelihood of attracting organic traffic, as users tend to click on the top results.

Keyword research is a critical component of SEO. By identifying the keywords and phrases that your target audience uses when searching for products or services, you can optimize your website's content to align with their search intent. Tools like Google Keyword Planner and SEMrush can assist you in finding relevant keywords and assessing their search volume and competition.

Creating high-quality content is essential for SEO success. Develop informative and engaging blog posts, articles, and product descriptions that provide value to your target audience. Incorporate relevant keywords naturally within your content while maintaining readability and coherence. By consistently producing valuable content, you can establish your website as an authoritative source and improve your search engine rankings.

In addition to SEO, pay-per-click (PPC) advertising is a powerful tool for driving targeted traffic to your e-commerce website. With PPC, you bid on keywords and display ads in search engine results or on relevant websites. You only pay when a user clicks on your ad, making it a cost-effective strategy.

Platforms like Google Ads and Bing Ads offer robust PPC advertising solutions. They allow you to set your budget, create compelling ad copy, and target specific demographics, locations, and devices. By crafting persuasive ad campaigns, optimizing landing pages, and monitoring performance metrics, you can maximize the effectiveness of your PPC campaigns and drive qualified traffic to your e-commerce website.

HARNESSING THE POWER OF SOCIAL MEDIA MARKETING

In the realm of e-commerce, social media has revolutionized the way businesses connect with their audience. With billions of active users across various platforms, social media marketing has emerged as a dynamic and influential tool for driving brand awareness, engaging customers, and boosting sales. In this chapter, we will explore the power of social media marketing and how you can harness its potential to grow your e-commerce business.

Social media platforms offer a multitude of opportunities to showcase your brand, engage with your target audience, and build a community around your products or services. By creating a strong social media presence, you can effectively communicate your brand's story, values, and offerings to a global audience.

The first step in social media marketing is to identify the platforms that align with your target audience. Whether it's Facebook, Instagram, Twitter, LinkedIn, or YouTube, each platform has its unique demographics and user behavior. Conduct market research and understand where your audience spends their time online. This will help you focus your efforts on the platforms that offer the greatest potential for reaching and engaging your target audience.

Creating compelling and shareable content is at the heart of successful social media marketing. Develop a content strategy that combines a mix of informative, entertaining, and visually appealing content. This could include engaging videos, eye-catching images, informative blog posts, customer testimonials, behind-the-scenes glimpses, and more. Tailor your content to resonate with your audience's preferences and interests.

Consistency is key in social media marketing. Regularly publish content and maintain an active presence on your chosen platforms. Develop a content calendar to ensure a steady flow of engaging posts. By staying consistent, you'll keep your brand top of mind and encourage ongoing engagement with your audience.

Engagement is a fundamental aspect of social media marketing. Respond promptly to comments, messages, and mentions from your audience. Encourage conversation, ask questions, and seek feedback. Actively engage with influencers, industry experts, and relevant communities to expand your reach and build meaningful connections. By fostering two-way communication, you can build trust and loyalty among your audience.

Paid social media advertising offers powerful targeting options to reach specific segments of your audience. Platforms like Facebook Ads and Instagram Ads allow you to create highly targeted campaigns based on demographics, interests, behaviors, and more. By strategically allocating your advertising budget and crafting persuasive ad content, you can amplify your reach, attract new customers, and drive conversions.

LEVERAGING EMAIL MARKETING FOR E-COMMERCE SUCCESS

In an era dominated by social media and instant messaging, email marketing remains a highly effective strategy for e-commerce businesses to engage with their audience, nurture relationships, and drive sales. In this chapter, we will explore the power of email marketing and how you can leverage it to achieve e-commerce success.

Email marketing allows you to communicate directly with your customers and prospects, delivering personalized and targeted messages to their inbox. It offers a unique opportunity to build a long-term relationship with your audience and keep your brand top of mind. By harnessing the potential of email marketing, you can drive repeat purchases, increase customer loyalty, and generate revenue for your e-commerce business.

The first step in email marketing is building a high-quality email list. Encourage website visitors to subscribe to your newsletter by offering exclusive content, discounts, or incentives. Use opt-in forms strategically placed on your website and landing pages to capture leads. Ensure that your subscribers have given explicit consent to receive emails from you to comply with privacy regulations.

Segmentation is a key aspect of successful email marketing. Divide your email list into different segments based on demographics, purchase history, engagement levels, or other relevant factors. This allows you to deliver tailored messages to specific segments, increasing the relevance and impact of your emails. Personalization plays a crucial role in engaging subscribers and driving conversions.

Craft compelling email content that resonates with your audience. Consider their interests, pain points, and preferences when creating email campaigns. Whether it's informative newsletters, product updates, exclusive offers, or personalized recommendations, deliver value in every email. Use persuasive copy, eye-catching visuals, and clear calls-to-action to drive engagement and conversions.

Automation is a game-changer in email marketing. Implement automated email workflows triggered by specific actions or events, such as welcome emails, abandoned cart reminders, post-purchase follow-ups, or re-engagement campaigns. Automation allows you to deliver timely and relevant messages to your subscribers, nurturing them along the customer journey.

Testing and analytics are essential for optimizing your email marketing efforts. A/B testing different subject lines, content variations, or calls-to-action can provide valuable insights into what resonates with your audience. Monitor email open rates, click-through rates, conversion rates, and other metrics to assess the effectiveness of your campaigns and make data-driven improvements.

Email marketing offers various opportunities for e-commerce businesses to engage their audience and drive conversions. Here are some additional strategies and techniques to enhance your email marketing efforts:

Personalized Product Recommendations: Leverage customer data and purchase history to provide personalized product recommendations in your emails. By analyzing past purchases and understanding customer preferences, you can suggest relevant products that align with their interests and needs. This personalized approach increases the chances of driving additional sales and improving customer satisfaction.

Exclusive Offers and Promotions: Use email marketing as a platform to deliver exclusive offers, discounts, and promotions to your subscribers. Create a sense of urgency by incorporating limited-time deals or flash sales. By making your subscribers feel special and providing them with exclusive benefits, you can drive traffic to your e-commerce website and increase conversion rates.

Customer Reviews and Testimonials: Incorporate customer reviews and testimonials in your email campaigns. Social proof plays a crucial role in influencing purchasing decisions. Include positive reviews and testimonials that highlight the benefits and quality of your products or services. This builds trust and credibility, encouraging subscribers to make a purchase.

Abandoned Cart Recovery: Implement automated emails to target users who have abandoned their shopping carts. Remind them of the items they left behind and offer incentives to complete the purchase, such as free shipping or a discount. These gentle reminders can significantly increase the likelihood of converting abandoned carts into completed purchases.

Post-Purchase Follow-ups: After a customer makes a purchase, send a follow-up email to express your appreciation and gather feedback. This shows that you value their business and provides an opportunity to address any concerns or issues. Additionally, consider including relevant cross-sell or upsell recommendations based on their recent purchase, encouraging repeat purchases.

Nurturing Drip Campaigns: Develop automated drip campaigns that deliver a series of emails to nurture leads and guide them through the customer journey. Start with a welcome email that introduces your brand and sets expectations. Subsequent emails can provide additional information, educational content, or relevant product recommendations. This automated nurturing process keeps your brand engaged with potential customers and increases the likelihood of conversion over time.

Mobile Optimization: With the majority of emails being opened on mobile devices, it is crucial to optimize your email designs for mobile responsiveness. Ensure that your emails display correctly on various screen sizes, load quickly, and have clear and easily clickable CTAs. Mobile-optimized emails provide a seamless user experience and increase the chances of engagement and conversion.

Throughout this chapter, we have explored the various aspects of email marketing for e-commerce businesses. By implementing these strategies, you can effectively engage your audience, drive conversions, and foster long-term customer relationships. Email marketing remains a powerful tool in your marketing arsenal, allowing you to connect directly with your customers and maximize the potential of your e-commerce business.

MAXIMIZING CONVERSIONS WITH CONVERSION RATE OPTIMIZATION

In the world of e-commerce, driving traffic to your website is only half the battle. The ultimate goal is to convert that traffic into paying customers. Conversion rate optimization (CRO) is the process of maximizing the percentage of website visitors who take a desired action, such as making a purchase, signing up for a newsletter, or filling out a form. In this chapter, we will delve into the art and science of CRO and explore effective strategies to maximize conversions for your e-commerce business.

Understanding Your Audience: To optimize conversions, you need to have a deep understanding of your target audience. Conduct thorough market research and analyze customer data to gain insights into their demographics, preferences, motivations, and pain points. This knowledge will help you tailor your website experience to their needs and create compelling calls-to-action that resonate with them.

Clear and Compelling Calls-to-Action: A clear and compelling call-to-action (CTA) is crucial for driving conversions. Your CTAs should be prominently displayed, visually appealing, and use persuasive language. Consider using action verbs and creating a sense of urgency to prompt immediate action. Test different variations of CTAs to identify what resonates best with your audience.

Streamlined Checkout Process: The checkout process is a critical stage where many potential customers abandon their purchases. Streamlining and simplifying the checkout process is essential for maximizing conversions. Eliminate unnecessary steps, minimize form fields, and provide clear instructions. Offer guest checkout options and provide multiple secure payment methods to accommodate different customer preferences.

Social Proof and Trust Signals: Building trust is crucial in e-commerce. Incorporate social proof elements such as customer reviews, testimonials, ratings, and trust badges on your website. These signals reassure potential customers about the reliability and quality of your products or services, increasing their confidence to make a purchase.

A/B Testing and Data Analysis: A/B testing involves comparing two variations of a web page or element to determine which one performs better in terms of conversions. Test different layouts, colors, headlines, product descriptions, and other elements to identify the most effective combination. Collect and analyze data to make data-driven decisions and continually optimize your website for higher conversion rates.

Personalization and Dynamic Content: Personalizing the user experience based on individual preferences and behaviors can significantly impact conversions. Leverage customer data to deliver personalized product recommendations, customized messaging, and targeted offers. Dynamic content that adapts to the user's browsing history or previous interactions creates a more personalized and engaging experience.

Mobile Optimization: With the rise of mobile devices, optimizing your website for mobile users is essential for maximizing conversions. Ensure that your website is mobile-responsive, loads quickly, and provides a seamless browsing and shopping experience across various devices. Mobile optimization improves user experience and eliminates barriers that may hinder conversions.

In this chapter, we have explored key strategies and techniques to maximize conversions through conversion rate optimization. By implementing these strategies and continually testing and analyzing your website's performance, you can optimize the user experience, reduce friction, and drive more conversions for your e-commerce business.

THE POWER OF INFLUENCER MARKETING FOR E-COMMERCE SUCCESS

Influencer marketing has become a powerful force in the world of e-commerce, offering a unique opportunity for businesses to tap into the reach, credibility, and influence of popular individuals in their respective niches. In this chapter, we will explore the power of influencer marketing and how you can leverage it to drive brand awareness, increase credibility, and boost sales for your e-commerce business.

Identifying the Right Influencers: The success of influencer marketing hinges on partnering with the right influencers who align with your brand and target audience. Conduct thorough research to identify influencers whose values, interests, and audience demographics match your business objectives. Look for influencers with a genuine and engaged following, as authenticity is key to building trust with their audience.

Building Authentic Relationships: Influencer marketing is about more than a simple transactional exchange. It's about building authentic relationships with influencers. Take the time to genuinely connect with influencers, understand their interests, and demonstrate how your brand can provide value to their audience. Building these relationships fosters mutual trust and increases the likelihood of a successful partnership.

Developing a Collaborative Strategy: Collaborate with influencers to develop a tailored influencer marketing strategy that aligns with your goals. Determine the type of content they will create, the platforms they will use, and the key messages you want to convey. Encourage influencers to infuse their unique voice and style into the content, ensuring authenticity and resonance with their audience.

Creative Content Creation: Influencers are known for their creativity and ability to captivate their audience. Leverage their expertise by giving them creative freedom to develop engaging and compelling content. Whether it's product reviews, sponsored posts, unboxing videos, or behind-the-scenes glimpses, allow influencers to showcase your products or services in an authentic and creative way that resonates with their audience.

Tracking and Measuring Performance: Establish key performance indicators (KPIs) to track the success of your influencer marketing campaigns. Monitor metrics such as engagement rates, reach, website traffic, and conversions to assess the impact of the collaboration. Use tracking links or unique discount codes to attribute sales directly to influencer-driven efforts. This data will help you evaluate the ROI of your influencer partnerships and make informed decisions for future collaborations.

Compliance and Disclosure: It is essential to comply with the Federal Trade Commission (FTC) guidelines and ensure proper disclosure of sponsored content. Work with influencers to ensure they clearly disclose their partnership with your brand in accordance with the regulations. Transparency builds trust with both the influencer's audience and regulatory bodies, protecting your brand's reputation.

Micro-Influencers and Niche Markets: Consider partnering with micro-influencers who have a smaller but highly engaged and targeted audience. Micro-influencers often have a deeper connection with their followers and can yield higher engagement rates. They also tend to be more cost-effective, making them a valuable option for targeting niche markets or specific product categories.

Throughout this chapter, we have explored the power of influencer marketing and how it can propel your e-commerce business to new heights. By strategically partnering with influencers, building authentic relationships, and creating engaging content, you can amplify your brand's reach, gain credibility, and drive conversions.

HARNESSING THE POWER OF SOCIAL MEDIA MARKETING FOR E-COMMERCE

Social media has revolutionized the way we connect, communicate, and consume content. It has also become a powerful platform for e-commerce businesses to reach and engage their target audience. In this chapter, we will explore the power of social media marketing and how you can harness it to drive brand awareness, foster customer engagement, and generate sales for your e-commerce business.

Choosing the Right Social Media Platforms: With a plethora of social media platforms available, it's essential to choose the ones that align with your target audience and business objectives. Conduct market research to identify where your target audience spends their time online. Focus your efforts on platforms like Facebook, Instagram, Twitter, LinkedIn, or TikTok, depending on your audience demographics and preferences.

Developing a Social Media Strategy: A well-defined social media strategy is crucial for achieving success. Set clear goals and objectives that align with your overall business objectives. Determine the type of content you will create, the frequency of posting, and the key messages you want to convey. Tailor your strategy to each platform, considering their unique features, audience expectations, and content formats.

Building an Engaged Community: Social media is all about building communities and fostering engagement. Create content that encourages conversations, asks questions, and prompts interactions with your audience. Respond promptly to comments, messages, and mentions to show that you value and appreciate your community. Engaging with your audience strengthens relationships and builds brand loyalty.

Visual Storytelling: Visual content is king on social media. Leverage the power of compelling visuals to tell your brand story and captivate your audience. Use high-quality images, videos, infographics, and animations that align with your brand's aesthetic and resonate with your target audience. Visual storytelling helps grab attention, evoke emotions, and leave a lasting impression.

Influencer Collaborations: We discussed the power of influencer marketing in a previous chapter, and social media platforms are ideal for influencer collaborations. Partnering with influencers allows you to tap into their established audience and leverage their influence to promote your products or services. Collaborating with influencers amplifies your reach and credibility, driving brand awareness and conversions.

Paid Advertising: Social media platforms offer robust advertising capabilities to reach a wider audience and target specific demographics or interests. Utilize paid advertising options such as Facebook Ads, Instagram Ads, or promoted tweets to expand your reach, drive website traffic, and generate conversions. Develop targeted campaigns with compelling ad creatives and clear calls-to-action to maximize results.

Social Listening and Analytics: Monitor social media conversations and sentiment surrounding your brand. Social listening allows you to understand customer perceptions, identify trends, and respond to feedback or inquiries promptly. Additionally, leverage social media analytics to track the performance of your campaigns, measure engagement metrics, and identify opportunities for improvement.

By leveraging the power of social media marketing, you can establish a strong online presence, connect with your target audience, and drive business growth for your e-commerce venture.

MASTERING CUSTOMER RETENTION AND LOYALTY STRATEGIES

In the competitive world of e-commerce, acquiring new customers is important, but retaining existing customers and fostering loyalty is equally essential for long-term success. In this chapter, we will explore effective strategies to master customer retention and loyalty, ensuring that your e-commerce business thrives by cultivating strong relationships with your customers.

Exceptional Customer Service: Providing exceptional customer service is the foundation of customer retention. Aim to exceed customer expectations at every touchpoint. Respond promptly to inquiries, address concerns, and resolve issues with a positive attitude. Personalize interactions and make customers feel valued and appreciated. Exceptional customer service fosters trust, satisfaction, and loyalty.

Personalization and Segmentation: Personalization goes beyond addressing customers by their names. Utilize customer data to segment your audience based on preferences, purchase history, and behavior. Deliver personalized product recommendations, tailored offers, and relevant content. Personalization enhances the customer experience, strengthens engagement, and increases the likelihood of repeat purchases.

Loyalty Programs: Implement a well-designed loyalty program to reward and incentivize repeat purchases. Offer exclusive discounts, special promotions, early access to new products, or loyalty points that customers can accumulate and redeem. Loyalty programs encourage customers to choose your brand over competitors and cultivate a sense of belonging and appreciation.

Email Marketing for Retention: Leverage email marketing as a powerful tool for customer retention. Develop targeted email campaigns that nurture and engage existing customers. Send personalized product recommendations, exclusive offers, and relevant content based on their preferences and purchase history. Use automated email workflows to re-engage inactive customers and win them back.

Social Media Engagement: Maintain an active presence on social media to engage and connect with your customers. Respond to comments, messages, and reviews promptly. Encourage user-generated content by running contests or featuring customer testimonials. Engaging with customers on social media builds relationships, enhances brand loyalty, and generates positive word-of-mouth.

Surprise and Delight: Surprise and delight your customers with unexpected gestures and personalized experiences. Send handwritten thank-you notes, surprise gifts, or exclusive sneak peeks of upcoming products. These small acts of appreciation create memorable experiences and deepen the emotional connection with your brand.

Continuous Feedback and Improvement: Actively seek feedback from your customers to understand their needs, preferences, and pain points. Conduct surveys, analyze reviews, and listen to their suggestions. Use this feedback to improve your products, services, and overall customer experience. By showing that you value their input, you build trust and loyalty.

By implementing effective customer retention and loyalty strategies, you can create a community of loyal customers who not only make repeat purchases but also become brand advocates, promoting your business to their networks.

THE POWER OF DATA-DRIVEN DECISION MAKING IN E-COMMERCE

In the digital age, data is abundant and holds tremendous potential for shaping business strategies and driving growth. In this chapter, we will explore the power of data-driven decision making in e-commerce and how you can harness the insights derived from data to make informed, strategic choices for your business.

Collecting Relevant Data: The first step in data-driven decision making is to collect relevant data from various sources. This includes customer data, website analytics, sales figures, social media metrics, and market research. Implement tools and technologies that help you gather and consolidate data efficiently. Ensure compliance with privacy regulations and prioritize data security.

Data Analysis and Visualization: Once you have collected data, it's crucial to analyze and interpret it effectively. Use analytics tools to uncover patterns, trends, and correlations within the data. Visualize the data through charts, graphs, and dashboards to make it more accessible and understandable. Data visualization enables you to communicate insights to stakeholders and make informed decisions.

Customer Segmentation and Targeting: Utilize data to segment your customer base into distinct groups based on demographics, behaviors, preferences, and purchasing patterns. This segmentation helps you target specific customer segments with tailored marketing campaigns, personalized recommendations, and relevant offers. By understanding your customers at a granular level, you can optimize your marketing efforts and maximize conversions.

Pricing and Promotion Optimization: Data-driven decision making can optimize pricing strategies and promotional activities. Analyze pricing data, competitor pricing, and customer buying behaviors to determine the optimal price points for your products or services. Use data to identify the most effective promotional channels, timing, and messaging to maximize the impact of your promotions.

Inventory Management and Demand Forecasting: Data-driven insights can optimize inventory management and demand forecasting. Analyze historical sales data, seasonality, and market trends to anticipate demand patterns accurately. Use this information to optimize your inventory levels, minimize stockouts, and reduce carrying costs. Data-driven demand forecasting ensures that you can meet customer demands while avoiding excess inventory.

Conversion Rate Optimization (CRO): Data plays a pivotal role in CRO strategies. Analyze website and conversion data to identify bottlenecks, optimize user experience, and enhance conversion rates. A/B testing different elements such as layouts, colors, copy, and CTAs based on data-driven insights can lead to significant improvements in conversion rates and overall performance.

Predictive Analytics and Future Planning: Leverage predictive analytics to forecast future trends, customer behaviors, and market dynamics. By analyzing historical data, you can make educated predictions about future outcomes. Use these predictions to inform your strategic planning, product development, marketing campaigns, and expansion initiatives.

By embracing data-driven decision making, you can unlock powerful insights that drive business growth and competitive advantage. Data empowers you to make informed choices, optimize operations, and meet customer expectations in a rapidly evolving e-commerce landscape.

RETAINING CUSTOMERS AND FOSTERING CUSTOMER LOYALTY

In the competitive e-commerce landscape, customer retention is vital for sustained business growth and profitability. In this chapter, we will explore effective strategies to retain customers and foster long-term loyalty, turning them into brand advocates and repeat purchasers.

Deliver an Exceptional Post-Purchase Experience: The post-purchase experience is a crucial opportunity to leave a lasting impression on your customers. Send personalized order confirmation and shipping notifications to keep them informed about their purchase. Follow up with a thank-you email or post-purchase survey to gather feedback and show appreciation for their business. Providing a seamless and delightful post-purchase experience strengthens the bond with your customers.

Implement Email Marketing Campaigns: Email marketing is a powerful tool for nurturing customer relationships and driving repeat purchases. Segment your email list based on customer behavior and preferences. Send personalized product recommendations, exclusive offers, and relevant content to keep customers engaged and encourage them to return to your website. Use automation to trigger targeted emails based on specific customer actions or milestones, such as abandoned carts or birthdays.

Loyalty Programs and Rewards: Implement a loyalty program to incentivize repeat purchases and reward customer loyalty. Offer exclusive discounts, early access to new products, or special perks for members. Create tiers or point-based systems that allow customers to accumulate rewards over time. Communicate the benefits and value of your loyalty program to encourage sign-ups and active participation.

Provide Proactive Customer Support: Exceptional customer support goes beyond resolving issues—it involves being proactive in anticipating and addressing customer needs. Offer live chat support to assist customers in real-time. Provide self-help resources, FAQs, and knowledge bases to empower customers to find answers independently. Implement a system to track and resolve customer complaints and feedback promptly. Proactive customer support builds trust and enhances loyalty.

Personalize the Customer Experience: Personalization plays a crucial role in customer retention. Utilize customer data to personalize communications, product recommendations, and offers based on their preferences and purchase history. Address customers by name in emails and tailor content to their interests. Create personalized shopping experiences that make customers feel valued and understood.

Encourage User-Generated Content: User-generated content (UGC) is a powerful way to foster customer loyalty and drive engagement. Encourage customers to share their experiences through reviews, testimonials, and social media posts. Run contests or campaigns that encourage customers to create and share content related to your brand. Showcase UGC on your website and social media platforms to build trust and authenticity.

Continuously Improve and Innovate: Stay ahead of the competition by continuously improving and innovating your products, services, and customer experience. Gather feedback from customers through surveys, reviews, and social media listening. Actively seek opportunities to enhance your offerings and address pain points. Demonstrate your commitment to providing the best possible experience to keep customers coming back.

By implementing effective customer retention strategies, you can foster long-term loyalty and transform customers into brand advocates. Delivering an exceptional post-purchase experience, utilizing email marketing campaigns, implementing loyalty programs, providing proactive customer support, personalizing the customer experience, encouraging user-generated content, and continuously improving and innovating are essential strategies for retaining customers and driving repeat business.

CONCLUSION

In this book, we have embarked on a journey through the dynamic and ever-evolving world of e-commerce marketing strategy. We explored various aspects, from building a strong brand presence to driving traffic, maximizing conversions, fostering customer loyalty, and harnessing the power of data analytics. Each chapter provided valuable insights, practical strategies, and real-world examples to help you navigate the complexities of e-commerce and achieve success.

By the end of this book, you have gained a comprehensive understanding of the essential elements that contribute to a thriving e-commerce business. You have learned how to craft a compelling brand story, optimize your website for search engines, leverage social media platforms, implement effective marketing campaigns, scale your business, maximize conversions, retain customers, and harness the power of data analytics. Armed with this knowledge, you are well-equipped to tackle the challenges and seize the opportunities that come your way.

Remember that success in e-commerce requires continuous learning, adaptation, and innovation. Stay abreast of the latest trends, technologies, and consumer behaviors. Embrace a customer-centric approach and always strive to exceed their expectations. Test, measure, and iterate your strategies based on data-driven insights. And most importantly, never lose sight of the value of building genuine connections with your customers.

As you embark on your e-commerce journey, remember that it is a process of growth and evolution. Embrace the journey and the lessons it brings. Be resilient, agile, and willing to adapt. With the right strategies, a customer-centric mindset, and a passion for delivering value, you have the power to create a thriving e-commerce business that stands the test of time.

Congratulations on completing this journey through the world of e-commerce marketing strategy. Armed with the knowledge, strategies, and resources shared in this book, you are well-equipped to embark on a successful e-commerce journey. Remember that success comes with dedication, perseverance, and a continuous drive for improvement. Embrace the challenges, seize the opportunities, and create a thriving e-commerce business that makes a lasting impact. Best of luck on your e-commerce adventure!

www.ingramcontent.com/pod-product-compliance
Lightning Source LLC
Chambersburg PA
CBHW070851220526
45466CB00005B/1958